I Am a Part

Dona Herweck Rice

Publishing Credits

Rachelle Cracchiolo, M.S.Ed., *Publisher*
Conni Medina, M.A.Ed., *Managing Editor*
Nika Fabienke, Ed.D., *Content Director*
Véronique Bos, *Creative Director*
Shaun N. Bernadou, *Art Director*
Seth Rogers, *Editor*
John Leach, *Assistant Editor*
Courtney Roberson, *Senior Graphic Designer*

Image Credits: All images from iStock and/or Shutterstock.

Teacher Created Materials
5301 Oceanus Drive
Huntington Beach, CA 92649-1030
www.tcmpub.com
ISBN 978-1-4938-9865-7
© 2019 Teacher Created Materials, Inc.

I am a part of

my  .

team

I am a part of

my  .

team

I am a part of

my  .

team

I am a part of

my  .

team

I am a part of

my  .

team

I am a part of

my  .

team

I am a part of

my  .

team

I am a part of

my  .

team

I am a part of

my  .

team

I am a part of

my  .

team

High-Frequency Words

New Words

am			my

part

Review Words

a			I

of